LA LLORONA AND OTHER TALES OF THE AMERICAN SOUTHWEST

A full length play

By Elise Forier Edie

This play is dedicated to Wenda and Barb, who believed I could
write it
And to Meg Nolan, who asked me to

SETTING

"La Llorona" takes place in the late 1990's in various locations in a Southwestern American city

La Llorona "The Lady Who Weeps" is a traditional figure in southwestern Mexican American folklore. As the story goes, a young woman of Mexican-Indian descent fell in love with a Spanish nobleman, who had two children with her and then decided to marry a woman of his own class. When his new wife proved childless, he asked La Llorona to give up her children to him, but in her rage and grief, she drowned them in the river instead. Later, she went mad and died. When she came to the gates of heaven, St. Peter refused to let her enter without her children. La Llorona returned to earth where she haunts the riverbeds still, searching and crying for her lost children. She is said to have driven men mad, stolen babies and many people swear straight faced they have heard her howling in the middle of the night and it chilled their blood.

This play is best served by a unit set. I imagine several levels, decorated perhaps to look like the home altars one finds in Mexico and the southwestern United States. They are elaborately beautiful constructions of found objects – bottle caps, greeting cards, sea shells and so forth. Candles should predominate as should pictures of the Madonna and child. Tia should never leave the stage, until near the end of the play. As the storyteller, she should sit in some central place, rather like a Madonna herself.

The play is written to be continuous action, with no act break or clunky scene changes.

LIST OF CHARACTERS

6 women (5 Latinas, 1 Anglo-American), 4-5 men (Latinos)

In the land of myth:

LA LLORONA, female, dancer, any age

THE MASKED MAN***, male, dancer, any age

In el barrio:

ANDREA, a high school student, Latina female, 15 years old

ESME, her cousin, Latina female, 16 years old

TIA, their aunt, Latina female, 30's-40's

TITO, cousin to Andrea & Esme, son of Tia, Latino male,14 years old

MONICA, lives with Tia, has a baby by Tito's brother, friend to Esme and Andrea, Latina female, 17 years old

PAPA, Tia's brother, Andrea's father, Latino male, 30's-40's

CARLOS, lives in el barrio, Latino male, any age

GILBERTO, a stranger to el barrio, Latino male, late teen - 20's

In the school:

DR PENNE, Anglo female, 30's-40's

> ***THE MASKED MAN can double as GILBERTO or PAPA, if necessary

AT RISE

(At rise. Lights on TIA in her chair.)

TIA: Do you know La Llorona? Like a dream, La Llorona. It is an old story and this is how it was told to me by my mother's mother and her mother's mother, who saw it happen.
(Music. LA LLORONA enters, masked, dancing as a young maid.)
She lived a long time ago, a beautiful young lady from a poor family. She was the most beautiful girl in the village, admired for her beauty, praised for her purity. And all this was so, until a handsome stranger, un hidalgo, a rich man, rode into town.

(THE MASKED MAN enters, exuding sexual vitality. He holds out his arm to LA LORONA. They circle one another as the musical tempo picks up. ANDREA enters, wearing her fiesta dress. She is a vibrant fifteen year old, exceptionally beautiful.)

ANDREA: Let us say I dreamed it
La estrella del corazón
Burning. A punta del luz
Dazzled with silver music.
Green leaves strung with
Fiesta flowers were not so bright
As my spirit
Shining in your hands

(The MASKED MAN and LA LLORONA dance, the steps formal, but full of feeling. He seduces her, leading her, until he catches sight of ANDREA. Then his attention fixes on her and he stalks her, circling, and she responds, while LA LLORONA looks on, beseeching.)

ANDREA : Let us say I danced it then
Swinging my limbs like a wheel
Turning the world, the mystery
El misterio, a dance

That sparkled from your eyes
To shine off my skin
Amante mio, my love

> *(ANDREA throws her arms around the MASKED MAN and
> he carries her from the stage. She is laughing with
> happiness. LA LLORONA follows, her arms reaching for
> the masked man. She reaches. She gives up, defeated.)*

TIA: Un hombre misterio rode into town. His face was fair. His
eyes flashed. His white teeth gleamed like stars, but La Llorona
could not see it. La Llorona was too sweet to imagine it. That he
was a wicked man and behind his beautiful face was the face of
Death!

> *(The MASKED MAN sweeps in. He holds out his hand to
> the crumpled LA LLORONA, who approaches tentatively,
> hopefully.)*

There is only one hombre who comes out of the desert, riding like a
king on his black horse.

> *(Their hands touch. Then the MASKED MAN laughs and
> turns on his heel, exiting. LA LLORONA shrieks at the
> betrayal.)*

Un hombre, no. El Diablo.

> *(Blackout. Silence. Giggles in the dark. Dim lights on
> ESME, ANDREA, MONICA and TITO, as children, huddled
> in sleeping bags. They shiver and shriek as ESME speaks.)*

ESME: And Tia told me you can hear her, down by the river,
howling and crying. You can hear her when the moon is full, and on
El Dia de los Muertos. And sometimes, you can see her. You will be
walking after sundown, and you know that you should be home.
And maybe you are even running because you are worried that La
Llorona is waiting for you down by the river. And you will look
behind you, because you hear a noise and that is when you RUN
RIGHT INTO HER!

*(ESME has whipped out a flashlight and made her face into
an eerie, grinning mask. The other children scream,
ANDREA most of all.)*

ESME: She has the face of a devil! And eyes like flames! And her
teeth are dripping with blood!

ANDREA:EEEEEEE! Eeeeeee!
*(ANDREA has buried her face in her sleeping bag in an
ecstasy of terror.)*

PAPA: (Off) Goddammit, would you kids pipe down.
(The CHILDREN hush ANDREA.)

ESME: (Whispering.) First, she grabs you by the neck. Then … she
eats your brains.

MONICA: That's so sick.

ESME: You know what happens when someone eats your brains?
You can't feel it at all.

TITO: I can feel my brain.

ESME: No, you can't. You got no nerves up there.

TITO:I can. My brain is right—
(MONICA cuffs him.)

MONICA: Shut up, Tito, man.

ANDREA: Yeah, Tito, man.

ESME: So. La Llorona eats your brains, but you don't feel nothing,
except little by little, your body just shuts off. So she'll be eating
away and then all of a sudden you go numb because she, like, took a
bite of the feeling part of your brain. Or you'll, like, go blind,
because all of a sudden she took a bite of the seeing part of your

brain. Or maybe she eats the part where all your memories are stored and then you can't remember who you are.

TITO: Like a zombie, man.

ESME: Yeah. A zombie. And then you are the walking dead, and you ain't got no soul, because La Llorona has eaten that, too.

TITO: Dang, that is sick.

ANDREA: Turn the flashlight off, Esme.

ESME: Am I scaring you, Dre?

ANDREA: Just turn it off.

ESME: (Exorcist voice) Have you seen this face before? Have you looked on the face of La Llorona?

ANDREA: Stop it! Esme, I am really scared. Really.

MONICA: Tch. All that stuff's just dumb anyway.

TITO: No, it ain't!

ANDREA: Tata says it's true. She says La Llorona eats up all the bad children.

MONICA: It's just something los padres say to get the children home in time for supper. I don't believe a—

TITO: You better watch out, Monica—

ANDREA: (At the same time) La Llorona is gonna get you if you—

PAPA: (Off.) I said settle down you kids, or I'll settle everything for you.

ESME: (Pause.) It's true.

MONICA: Listen to you, Esme. "It's twue!" Who are you? Alice in Wonderland?

ESME: Shut up, Monica!
    (She throws a pillow. Giggles. MONICA throws one back. Soon a full fledged pillow fight ensues.)

PAPA: (Entering.) What did I say? What did I just say to you kids. (Silence.) Andrea?

ANDREA: Sorry.

PAPA: Sorry, what?

ANDREA: Sorry, sir.

PAPA: Now keep your mouths shut and go to sleep. (Exits.)

MONICA: Thorry, thir.
    (She and TITO laugh.)

ESME: Be quiet, Monica.

MONICA: Fine. Whatever.
    (The lights dim on everyone but ANDREA, who looks around, very frightened. She starts at a noise, then crams her sleeping bag under her chin.)

ANDREA: Esme? Esmeralda? Tito? Monica?
    (Cautiously, she creeps across the floor to where ESME was lying, but the stage is now empty. She panics, patting the dark floor.)
This isn't funny. I'm scared. Esmeralda? Papa? H-hello?

    (Suddenly, LA LLORONA is upon her. Long fingernails dig in her skin. ANDREA screams and runs away. Alone on stage, LA LLORONA turns and turns in a mad dance.)

TIA: Oh, she had been warned of course, about the ways of men. In her mind, she knew better. But madre! It was so romantic. Las cantatas de la fiesta became the beat of her heart, the song of the blood shivering in her veins. And she told herself the lies that all women whisper, when they are in love. "I will be different," she said. "I will change him. He looks at all the women in the village, but I will be so beautiful, and so good and so clever that he will see only me."

> *(ANDREA stands and reads from a notebook. She is now a fifteen year old, in TIA's house. ESME and MONICA sit nearby on a couch. TIA rocks in her chair. ESME cuddles a baby. ANDREA is nervous.)*

ANDREA: Let us say I dreamed it then
Un león del oro leaping
And I am in the tall grass
Watching, while tumbling flowers
Blossom in my belly—

MONICA: Whoo-girl! You are making me hot. Don't she make you hot, Esme?

ESME: Shut up, Monica. You're doing fine, Dre. Go on.

ANDREA: Let us say it was a dream of blossoms
And my love is a secret under glowing stars
How even now I watch you
And wish on you leaping
To catch me in velveted hands
And hold me so close, so close
Novio mio so close
That I will become real.

ESME: Dre, that is so money. It's money huh, Monica? What do you think, Tia?

TIA: I hope the mayor will be able to hear you, mi'ja. It is a very beautiful poem.

ANDREA: I wish you could come

TIA: I will be there in el alma. In my spirit.

ANDREA: Si. Entiendo.

TIA: But I must sleep, now. Remember Andrea, I am very proud.
    (She closes her eyes and drifts off.)

ESME: Chemotherapy. What good is it?

MONICA: (To ANDREA) I bet Gilbert likes your poem, huh?

ANDREA: I don't know. He's not coming, either.

ESME: What? You're winning the city high school poetry award
and he's not coming to hear you read for the mayor? That's not right,
Dre.

ANDREA: He says he has to work.

ESME: Monica, take the baby.

MONICA: Put her in her crib. And get your face out from in front
of the TV, my programs are on.

ESME: (Overlapping to ANDREA.) What's his phone number?

ANDREA: It's okay.

MONICA: Esme, why you got to be so uptight?

ESME: She wrote the poem for him. About like when you guys met
and stuff, right? The rodeo parade? (ANDREA nods.) So he should
be there.

MONICA: (Ignoring ESME.) Is Gilberto meeting you after the
award thing?

ANDREA: I don't know. He gets off work at eleven.

ESME: Monica, she—
    (MONICA gestures that ESME should shut up.)

MONICA: Okay. So if Gilberto has to work, we will take you out after the banquet. Right, Esme? We will get us some Boones Farm and some vodka and toast to Andrea Cuesta, La Artista del Barrio, eh? Just the girls. Who needs boys?

ANDREA: I have to ask my Papa.

ESME: Is the baby going with us, Monica?

MONICA: My nana will watch her.
    (GILBERTO enters. He is in another time and place and only addresses ANDREA.)

ESME: I still think someone should talk to him.

GILBERTO: I told you already. I got to work.

ESME: He must be stupid not to understand how important this is.

MONICA: Don't let Dre hear you say that.
    (Lights change, indicating another time and place as MONICA and ESME exit.)

ANDREA: I don't understand why you are mad at me. This is an honor, Gilberto.

GILBERTO: Dre—

ANDREA: Why? Why won't you come?

GILBERTO: I got work to do. I got bills to pay. Dang, it's just a prize for a poem.

ANDREA: What do you mean?

14

GILBERTO: You get, what? A plaque to hang on the wall? I mean, that's cool. But I got a real life to live.

ANDREA: Poetry makes your real life beautiful, Gilberto.

GILBERTO: No. You make my real life beautiful.

ANDREA: I do?

GILBERTO: Tch. I told you, babe. I see you like, at the fiesta de los vacqueros, standing by the dulces in your green dress. And my leg is busted and I didn't win nothing, even though I come all this way. But then, I see you, como una angelita. And I think, okay, maybe this trip ain't a total disaster. Because damn, they don't have nothing like you where I come from. Hey, don't pull away when I'm getting all horny and stuff.

ANDREA: I want you to come to the awards banquet, Gilberto. I want you to meet my papa. Maybe if he meets you, he'll let me—

GILBERTO: Look. I can come get you after work. The award-thing will be over, but—

ANDREA: I already told Papa I was going out with Monica.

GILBERTO: So? Monica's cool. We'll sneak off. And we can still celebrate even though I'm missing the mayor and all.

ANDREA: Okay.

GILBERTO: I'll come by Monica's at midnight.

ANDREA: Her nana and tata will see you.

GILBERTO: Then I'll meet you at the park.

ANDREA: But—

GILBERTO: Come on, Dre. Be nice.
(He kisses her.)

ANDREA: I'm sorry, but you—

GILBERTO: Be sweet.

(He tries to kiss her again but she pulls away.)

ANDREA: I have to go home. My papa—

GILBERT: (Hands off.) Yeah, your papa. Run along, little girl. My tough luck to be dating a sixteen year old.

ANDREA: Fifteen. I'm fifteen. I'm sorry.

GILBERTO: It's not your fault. It's mine.
(He dismisses her with a wave. They exit as lights change. Lights up on DR PENNE, a school counselor, in her office. ESME waits outside her door. TITO stands by her desk.)

DR PENNE: (On the telephone) I do not believe we have ever had a District Poetry Award Winner in the history of Central South High. We all think it's a wonderful indication of the positive direction our school is going.

TITO: Miss, I'm here with the health forms.

DR PENNE: Tito could you hold one second?
(Into the phone)
Ellen Penne. P-E-N-N-E. Yes. I'm the counselor here, in charge of special programs. Right. Thank you. When is the article coming out? Great. Well, call me if you have any other questions. Good bye.
(Hangs up)
Okay, Tito. Did your mother sign the forms this time?

TITO: Sure.

DR PENNE: And did you tell her I needed to speak to her?

TITO: She ain't feeling too good, Miss.

DR PENNE: Well, is there any adult who can speak on your behalf? I'm worried about this experimentation with your medication, the mood swings, the—

TITO: I got all that stuff worked out.

DR PENNE: Excuse me?

TITO: I got all that shit—excuse me, stuff—worked out with my meds, Miss. Don't worry about nothing. It's like, handled.

DR PENNE: Would you at least have your mother call me?

TITO: She don't speak English all that well.

DR PENNE: I can find someone to translate.

TITO: Yeah. Can I be excused, please?

DR PENNE: Tito. Do you really need to ask?
       (He exits and almost bumps into ESME.)

TITO: What you doing in the counselor's office, Alien Breath?

ESME: Why don't you shut up and take a pill, Tito?

DR PENNE: Who's next?

ESME: It's me, Miss.

DR PENNE: Esmeralda Trujillo. I'm glad you came. Do you know who I am?

ESME: You are the Miss who entered my cousin Andrea's poem in the City Contest.

DR PENNE: Is Andrea your cousin? How nice. Yes. I am the counselor in charge of special programs here.

ESME: Am I in some kind of trouble?

DR PENNE: Not at all.
>*(She takes a folder from her desk)*
Quite the contrary, actually. I called you in here because you are very gifted. Your math aptitude scores are off the charts. Did you know that?

ESME: I like math.

DR PENNE: Tell me, Esmeralda. What are your plans after you graduate? (ESME shrugs) Do you want to go to college?

ESME: I … I want to be a doctor. But. That's stupid, right?

DR PENNE: I don't think so.

ESME: I guess I never said it out loud before. It's embarrassing.

DR PENNE: I think it's entirely possible.

ESME: You do?

DR PENNE: I think you're exactly the kind of student any college would be glad to have. And now's the time to start getting ready. Your Junior year can be very crucial when it comes to admissions. Good colleges like to see their prospective students challenging themselves, testing their limits. What do you think about that?

ESME: I work hard in all my classes, and I—

DR PENNE: Here's the thing. I recently got funding to start an Advanced Placement program after school. I want you to be in it, Esmeralda. I think you're an excellent candidate.

ESME: After school? Like a club?

DR PENNE: It would be a class. You'd take accelerated math and science and some college credit. There are lots of universities looking for bright young women like you, but a course like this can make you seem like a really great prospect for scholarships.
(ESME looks uncomfortable)
What's wrong?

ESME: The program is after school.

DR PENNE: The classes go until seven o'clock five days a week. That's what you'll need, to get up to speed.

ESME: I need to be at home to help my family. My tia—my aunt—has cancer. In her liver and her blood. And everybody else works, and with my tia so sick … she has children … I need to be at home.

DR PENNE: Well, it might be worth it for your family to find some outside help for your aunt. You stand to really benefit from these classes. It's not just the intellectual challenge. An opportunity like this could make a huge difference in your whole future.

ESME: Thank you. I will have to talk to my family. I will see you tonight though, huh?

DR PENNE: Tonight?

ESME: The banquet? Andrea's poem? The whole family is going.

DR PENNE: Of course. I'm looking forward to it. Meanwhile, please think about the Advanced Placement program. I would like so much to see someone with your potential really succeed.
(ESME exits. Lights out on DR PENNE. Lights up on LA LLORONA, who dances. Music. CARLOS enters, dragging a plastic garbage bag full of pop cans. He sings, and has a beautiful voice. LA LLORONA catches sight of him and sneaks up.)

CARLOS
De colores.
De colores se vistan los campos en la primavera
De colores
De colores son los pajaritos que vienen de afuera
De colores

>*(LA LLORONA leaps in front of him with a snarl. He freezes, unable to breathe.)*

LA LLORONA: Cantate.
>*(She laughs as CARLOS shrinks away.)*

Cantate. Cantate!
>*(CARLOS flees, leaving his bag of cans behind him. LA LLORONA chases him, laughing.)*

Esta yo! Yo! Yo canto esta noche.

>*(LA LLORONA exits whooping, while MONICA enters, also whooping. ANDREA walks with her. They are dressed to the nines. MONICA carries a paper bag with a bottle inside.)*

MONICA: Where's the Juicy Fruit?

ANDREA: What?

MONICA: Man, I ain't going home without some gum, okay? I smell like Boone's Farm. Smell my breath.

ANDREA: Yuck, Monica. Don't be doing that.

MONICA : Hold on. There's a man under that tree. Fuck, I hope it's someone we know.

ANDREA: We know everyone in el barrio.

MONICA: Yeah, well … if they're drunk or they got a gun…or they're La Llorona…

20

ANDREA: You know what Tia told me? She said she heard La Llorona crying outside the window. And then the next day all the grass underneath it was dead. Like, she really had walked over the garden.

MONICA: Tch. Don't believe it. It was probably a cat fight and the cats just peed all over the grass. A cat can sound like a ghost. (Peers out.) Who is that? Maybe we should go.

ANDREA: Maybe it's Gilberto…

MONICA: Nah. It's Loco Carlos. Hey Carlos, man! (To ANDREA) Man, I wish there was some new guys around. I already done everybody on our block.

ANDREA: Monica.

MONICA: Don't look at me like that. I don't care.

ANDREA: Why?

MONICA: What do you mean, "Why?" Don't you and Gilbert do it?

ANDREA: No.

MONICA: I bet that ain't what he says.

ANDREA: It isn't true.

MONICA: Whatever. You keep yourself la virgin a little longer. Because it's not like you can just go back. And anyway, the first time is just embarrassing.

ANDREA: It is?

MONICA: Oh, my God. You're like, all naked and shit And he like … you know. He puts it inside you, right? I mean you know how babies are made? So. It's just … embarrassing. At first.

ANDREA: What about now?

MONICA: I don't know. I guess now it's embarrassing after.

ANDREA: Why?

MONICA: Because during, it's like he sees you, and he says nice things to you. But after … this is stupid, man. Listen to me. What do you want to know about this stuff for? You are la artistia. You are the writer. Tonight you read your poem for the Mayor.

ANDREA: I was so scared.

MONICA: I would be too, having all those white people hanging all over me. Why did the counselor lady have to hug you so much?

ANDREA: She was just really happy I won. But I'm glad you were there. And I'm glad you're here now.

MONICA: How come Esme ain't here with us?

ANDREA: She said "No," after I told her Gilberto was meeting us.

MONICA: Esme has a big, fat stick up her butt.

ANDREA: She just doesn't understand about Gilberto.

MONICA: Esme doesn't understand nothing. Even when she's a little girl she's like reading about dinosaurs, or some shit like that.
    (Looks off)
I think that's him coming.

    (LA LLORONA has crept back on stage as MONICA gets up to leave.)

ANDREA: Stay with me, Monica.

MONICA: What for?

ANDREA: I don't know. I'm scared. I always feel like I make Gilberto mad.

MONICA: What's to get mad about?

ANDREA: I don't know. Sometimes I feel like everyone's mad. But then I feel stupid all the time asking, "Do you still love me?" You know? Do you still love me, Monica?

MONICA: Are you for real? Dang girl. Have some more vodka.
        (GILBERTO enters)
Hey, Gilberto.

GILBERTO: Hey, Monica. Hey, Dre.

MONICA: You want a sip?

GILBERTO: What you got? Gatorade?

MONICA: Apple wine with vodka.

GILBERTO: That's nasty

MONICA: Shut up. No it ain't. In fact, listen the fuck up. I'm her chaperone, Gilberto. So you gotta tell me what you got planned for the chica here tonight, or I'm not letting her go nowhere with you.

ANDREA: Monica.

GILBERTO: (Playing along) I'm going to take her out for helados, Miss La Farga, and then escort her home.

MONICA: What time? You know you got to be punctual when it comes to Andrea or I'll tell her papa. You know Andrea's dad's a cop, right?

GILBERTO: I know what he is.

MONICA: So what time you escorting her back?

GILBERTO: Don't you have a baby to go home to?

MONICA: Fuck you. I'm leaving.
   (As she exits.)
Hey Loco Carlos, you wanna walk me home, man? I got a whole bag of pop cans at my house. And a six pack of Coca-cola.

(GILBERTO and ANDREA look at one another.)

GILBERTO: What?

ANDREA: How was work?

GILBERTO: Fine. You ready to go?

ANDREA: Where?

GILBERTO: My place.

ANDREA: You want to know about the poem?

GILBERTO: You read it, right? For the Mayor?

ANDREA: Yes.

GILBERTO: You look amazing in that dress. Come here.

ANDREA:Why?

GILBERTO: Because I'm going to kiss you. (They kiss.) Let's go.
   (He leads her offstage. LA LLORONA creeps after them.
   CARLOS enters carefully, and picks up his discarded bag of
   cans. He stares off where LA LLORONA exited. He
   frowns, worried.)

CARLOS: Cuidado, lady! La Llorona canta esta noche. La distingue, chica! Por favor.

MONICA: (Off) You coming, or not Carlos?

CARLOS: The lady...
(Lights change and come up on ESME and TIA.)

ESME: Finally, the children are asleep.

MONICA: (Off) Dumbass. No one is there. Come on!
(CARLOS exits.)

ESME: They splashed water everywhere in the bathroom. My clothes are wet.

TIA: Are you cold?

ESME: No. It feels nice. Are you cold?
(TIA shakes her head.)
Monica has a new lotion. Would you like some on your hands? It smells like vanilla and heaven.

(TIA holds out her hands and ESME sits across from her. She will rub lotion on TIA's arms and hands throughout the next scene.)

TIA: How was La Artista?

ESME: She was great. The Mayor gave her this beautiful plaque and the lady counselor gave a speech and she read her poem for everyone. It was nice. Only Uncle Rudolfo, he just stood there. I mean, he didn't hug her or nothing.

TIA: He is a man alone raising a daughter. He is a afraid to show weakness.

ESME: Tch. It's not weak to hug your daughter when she wins a prize from the Mayor.

TIA: How is your mama?

ESME: She works too much. I tell her, "Let me take a job after school," but she says, "You have to concentrate on your studies so you can get a scholarship to college."

TIA: Your mother is right. We would all be very proud if you went to the university.

ESME: I know. (Beat.) Tia. The school lady, the Miss who got Andrea into the poetry contest. She has told me that I qualify for a special program after school, to go to college early, in a way, take some advanced classes now, for free.

TIA: That is wonderful news, mi'ja!

ESME: Except. I will have to be at the school until seven or eight every night. I will not be able to see you as much, or help with the little ones. If I—

TIA: Mi'ja do you want to take this class?

ESME: Yes.

TIA: And it will help you get into college?

ESME: But I feel like I should be here with you.

TIA: I understand and I thank you. But you honor me more by using the gifts that God has given you. Don't you deserve our support, so that you can succeed? The family will find a way to care for me and the little ones. It's important, eh? For you?

ESME: Oh, tia ….

TIA: What?

ESME: It's just…I love you. What will I do when you are gone?

(Lights out on them. Dim lights on LA LLORONA, who dances sensuously in front of candles she has lit. We hear ANDREA.)

ANDREA:
I am real and you are here
Softly stroking there
My belly, my thighs, my hips
Everything seeking
How you touch me, you touch me—

(Lights reveal her with GILBERTO on a couch in the dark.)

GILBERTO: Let me do it to you.

(LA LLORONA freezes, listening closely.)

ANDREA: No.

GILBERTO: Come on. How long you gonna make me wait?

ANDREA: I'm scared.

GILBERTO: I told you, you got nothing to be afraid of.

ANDREA: My papa—

GILBERTO: He won't know.

ANDREA: He will if I have a baby.

GILBERTO: Can't happen the first time. This is the first time, right?

ANDREA: Yes.

GILBERTO: You'll like it. You'll love it.

ANDREA: Gilberto, I—

GILBERTO: It's all right. I love you. You know I love you, right?

ANDREA: I love you too and I want to make you happy—

GILBERTO: Good. Because right now I am in some serious pain.
Give me your hand, okay?

ANDREA: I—

GILBERTO: See? It doesn't bite, babe.

ANDREA: Am I touching it right?

GILBERTO: Right enough. It's not rocket science; it's not
complicated. It's just special. Let's make this night special.

ANDREA: It already was a special night.

GILBERTO: I know. I missed your poem, baby. So let me make it
up to you.

ANDREA: But I—

GILBERTO: You know why people write poems?

ANDREA: I—

GILBERTO: Shhh. Let me touch you, you'll see.

ANDREA: Just …

GILBERTO: Yeah?

ANDREA: Do I have to take off my clothes?

GILBERTO: I give up.
        (He gets up in disgust but LA LLORONA jumps in front of
        him, stopping him from getting too far away.)

28

ANDREA: Gilberto! I'm sorry. It's just I have never. Please come back. I'm just scared.

> *(LA LLORONA gestures. He turns to ANDREA. He really has no choice in the matter.)*

GILBERTO: It's all right. I'm a little worked up is all. But we can take it slow.

> *(Lights dim on them, but they remain on stage. GILBERT seduces ANDREA. This can be as done very theatrically, using only sound and shadows, or very graphically, if the director prefers. There should be no doubt in the audience's mind, however, about what is transpiring. LA LLORONA dances to the music of ANDREA and GILBERTO's lovemaking. Meanwhile, in another part of the stage, MONICA is on the phone.)*

MONICA: Your daughter needs to eat, okay? … David, please. I was not—I was not kissing no dude at no party! Okay? … He's lying. Anyway, what does that have to do with Vanessa, eh?...Listen,listen, I am out of food stamps … Maybe you come by more often, I wouldn't have to ask you for money every time I see you.

ANDREA: I will give you everything. I will do anything.

MONICA: I don't get why you got to get new tires again. You ride that truck so low right now everyone has to get out just to go over the railroad tracks. It's like you don't want anyone in the car but you. Why don't you do something for us?

ANDREA: I will. I will. And it will be like a dream. Is everything all right? Am I all right?

MONICA: No, she's not fine. She's dying.

ANDREA: Yes. And your face is like a marble angel above mine. Telling me aqui esta un area del peligro. Wait—

(ANDREA tries to get up, to stop what is happening, but LA LLORONA holds her down.)

MONICA: When are you coming home? Please, just when are you coming home? I need to talk to you. Not on the phone, in person.

ANDREA: Please I need to talk to you.

MONICA: That's the best you can do? That's it?

ANDREA: I love you. I'm scared—

MONICA: Whatever. Yeah, I love you to.

ANDREA: Do you love me? Do you love me?

MONICA: (Overlapping.) I'm sure Vanessa would love you too if she knew who you were. Idiote. Good bye.

(Lights fade on her despair.)

ANDREA: Something is wrong—

GILBERTO: Hush, please, God—

ANDREA: There's something wrong—

GILBERTO: No, no. You're perfect, this is good—

ANDREA: But I'm bleeding.

GILBERTO: Yeah, okay.

ANDREA: I'm bleeding.

(Lights dim on them. Lights up on TIA. ANDREA straightens her clothing and crosses to TIA as she talks. GILBERTO exits. ANDREA picks up MONICA's baby.

30

ESME enters and begins studying. MONICA enters with a box of make up samples.)

TIA: She loved him. She loved him. And she bore him children. And then one day, he did not come to call. And another day passed. And then another. And her heart was very troubled.

MONICA: Check it chicas. Free samples from the Avon lady.

ESME: Words do not express my excitement, Monica.

MONICA: It's some expensive shit. Want to try it?

ESME: No.

MONICA: Dre?

ANDREA: No.

MONICA: Why not? You want to look good for your man, don't you?

ANDREA: He hasn't called me. I don't know where he is.

ESME: Since when?

ANDREA: Since the poetry award.

ESME: But that was more than a week ago.

ANDREA: I know, Esme!

MONICA: One week, who cares?

ANDREA: I do.

MONICA: Tch. You gotta learn, chica. One week ain't nothing. Men. God gives them a dick, but that's it. They sure ain't got no brains. They can't remember nothing except football scores and some shit like that. They remember to call you maybe get you a birthday present? Forget it.

ANDREA: I can't be like you, Monica.

MONICA: Tch. Who can?

ANDREA: Yeah, right.

MONICA: Hey, I am in a good mood tonight, okay? This does not happen every day. You chicas be nice to me. Esme, let me do your face.

ESME: No.

MONICA: You gonna drag around your whole life looking like that?

ESME: Like what?

MONICA: Sit. Okay? Act like a girl for once in your life. Hold on, Dre. You're next.

ESME: This is stupid.

MONICA: Yeah, yeah. Monica is stupid and all that. Blah, blah. Someday you'll thank me. You'll finally get a date and you'll say, "Thank you Monica, for making me look beautiful." Okay. Hair. Esme, I got two words for you. Hair spray. You can read the label, right?

ESME: That stuff smells nasty.

MONICA: But your whole face gets ruined by bad hair.
        (She sprays ESME's hair.)

ESME: What did you just do?
        (MONICA continues the makeover, dragging out cosmetics and cotton balls and applying stuff to ESME's face.)

MONICA: Hold on. You gotta put foundation on your skin, okay? Some girls, they really got to cake it on because they got bad skin. But me? I'm okay. I get like zits and shit when I get my period? And then, I use a sponge to put it on. Trade secret, chica. You got to keep dabbing and dabbing. And you always go light. You got dark skin? You got to stay the hell out of the sun and go light.

ESME: I'm gonna look in the mirror. You're going to make me look like a clown, I know it.

MONICA: Tsss. Sit. I'm almost finished. Okay, lip liner. Go dark on the lips or dark on the eyes, but never both. That's what all the magazines say. One or the other. You, I'm gonna keep your eyes all inocente, and do just the lips. You put dark liner, and then fill in with brown or red. Now. You look very, very sexy, Esme. Don't she, Dre?

ESME: (Looking in a mirror.) Thank you, Monica.

MONICA: See? I am not such a dumb bitch after all. But let me tell you, that is just the basics. I just gave you enough to survive. I mean, I haven't even talked about the shit you got to do to get a smoky eye, or how to take off your mustache thingie, or what to do if your hair gets all frizzy. But man, I promise you, you could read magazines for a hundred years and still not know enough about making yourself look right. But you gotta start somewhere. I mean, every little bit helps. You're up next, Dre. Sit your butt down.

ANDREA: I don't want a makeover.

MONICA: I don't care. Let me do your face.

ANDREA: What for?

MONICA: So you'll look drop dead when he comes back. That's what you gotta do, babe. You gotta look amazing all the time because you never know when he's coming back. And it's a lot of work, let me tell you. But that's good. Because it gives you something to think about while you're waiting.

ANDREA: I don't want to wait.

MONICA: What else are you gonna do right now? Eh?
> *(The lights dim on MONICA and ESME, who will exit.*
> *ANDREA rises, puts the baby down and moves to a*
> *telephone. PAPA enters. It is another time and place; they*
> *are at ANDREA's home and her PAPA has returned from*
> *work.)*

PAPA: Goddamn these kids. Tagging on the park benches again.
Spray painting the bathroom walls. El barrio looks like a trash heap.
Last Saturday I painted over their filth. This Saturday, I'm going to
do it all over again--

ANDREA: I thought the neighborhood association treated those
walls with anti graffiti stuff.

PAPA: Those damn kids always find a way.

ANDREA: You shouldn't give up all your weekends to clean the
park, Papa.

PAPA: This is my home. I'm not giving up anything, that's just it. I
expect you to be there too, Andrea. You are an example to the rest
of the kids in this community.

ANDREA: Yes, Papa. (Beat.) Tito helped me hang the poetry
plaque on the wall.

PAPA: I hope he didn't crack the plaster.

ANDREA: He didn't.

PAPA: It's very nice, mi'ja.

ANDREA: Did you even like my poem, Papa?

PAPA: What is this—

ANDREA: You haven't said anything. Not one thing. Don't you like it?

PAPA: (Beat.) Who is it about?

ANDREA: What?

PAPA: It is a very … romantic poem. It makes me wonder. Is it about a boy? A boy from school?

ANDREA: It's…no. It's not about a boy--from school. The poem was … like a dream. Something I—

PAPA: It doesn't sound like a dream. You know what it sounds like? It sounds like you have been fooling around. And you know my rules, Andrea—

ANDREA: I know.

PAPA: You are too young for boys--

ANDREA: Yes, Papa.

PAPA: And if I find you have been seeing a boy behind my back, so help me—

ANDREA: I know! You've told me a million times.

PAPA: I make these rules to protect you, hija.

ANDREA: Yes, Papa.

PAPA: When I was your age, your grandfather had to give me permission to even speak to your mother.

ANDREA: You have told me. Many times. But not every boy is like the ones you see at work. There are nice boys—

PAPA: And are you seeing one? Andrea? Eh?

ANDREA: No, I guess I'm not. But Papa, your rules are so—

PAPA: Not a word about my rules. As long as you are in this house you follow them. And if I find you have disobeyed me. Hija. Since your mother died you are all I have. And I must protect you. There is so much out there, a system! Waiting to eat you up and spit you out—

ANDREA: Yes, Papa.

PAPA: A lot of attention was paid to you because of this poem. I do not want it to give you a swelled head. I haven't told you I am proud because I do not want you to become complacent. The only thing the world hands you, hija, is hardship. And the sooner you learn that, the better.

ANDREA: Yes, Papa,

PAPA: I need you to be smart. Be smart for me, Andrea.(She starts to exit) Where are you going?

ANDREA: I am going to Tia's to help with the children.

PAPA: I thought Esmeralda was helping.

ANDREA: She is in a science scholarship program. She works after school, now.

PAPA: See. Now, there is a thing you should have. Poetry is very nice, but a science scholarship is better.

ANDREA: I know, Papa. Thank you, Papa.

PAPA: Andrea…

ANDREA: Don't worry about me.

(Blackout on them. Lights up on DR PENNE, on the telephone in her office.)

DR PENNE: Michael, you would not believe the politics of public education. Everyone is competing for the same funds. Everyone thinks they're right. Everyone thinks their program is important. But it's not about tests. It's not. It's about one on one time in the classroom, and individual encouragement, and I am going to prove it. So. You have an in with the City Council, right? So what I need-
(ESME enters with a basket)
Can I call you right back? Thanks. Yes, I will. Good bye. (Hangs up.) Esmeralda. Tell me it's not a problem with the new program.

ESME: No. I brought something for you. A gift. These are my mother's tamales. They are really good—the best! And she wrote you a note to thank you.

DR PENNE: My goodness.

ESME: They take all day to make.

DR PENNE: Yes, I understand it's very complicated.

ESME: Miss, I am so happy in the new class. You know how if you are smart everyone makes fun of you? Before this program, I don't want to raise my hand in class because everyone rolls their eyes and whispers things. But now? In this new class? Everyone asks questions! Everyone does their homework! Is college like that?

DR PENNE: It can be.

ESME: Since I am a little girl, I have this secret dream that I will be a doctor. I see myself in the gown and mask, you know? At a table and there is a child laid out before me and she is very sick but I know how to save her life. I have the light of power in my hand, like a holy saint. And I put my finger on her heart and she opens her eyes, she breathes. This is what you have done for me. You have opened my eyes.

DR PENNE: (Gets up to hug her.) Esmeralda, hearing you say that makes my whole job worthwhile. Thank you.

ESME: There is going to be a fiesta in my neighborhood next month. Maybe you can come? My whole family will be there. They would very much like to meet you. You are like a celebrity. Can you come?

DR PENNE: I can try.

ESME: You can bring your husband, children. It is a party for everybody.

DR PENNE: Thank you. I'll keep that in mind.

ESME: Okay. I'll see you.

DR PENNE: Wait, Esmeralda. I hate to ask you this but…Will you see your cousin Andrea later on? If you do, could you tell her I'd like to speak to her? There's a new project she might be interested in.

ESME: Oh.

DR PENNE: Is there a problem?

ESME: Andrea is helping with my tia after school. She is very busy at home … because I am here.

DR PENNE: I see.

ESME: I'm sorry.

DR PENNE: Why? It's not your fault.

ESME: Isn't it?
 (ESME exits and DR PENNE sits for a moment.)

DR PENNE: Well, damn.

(Lights up on MONICA with her baby. Music plays and MONICA sings along. The baby cries. LA LLORONA dances to the music.)

MONICA: (To her baby) It's a beautiful day, chica. Birds are singing. Sun is shining. Look, I am Christina Aguilera! Check it out, baby. Damn, what are you crying for?
(CARLOS enters with his sack of pop cans)
Hey, Carlos. You come for the pop cans?

CARLOS: Baby.

MONICA: You got it. You want to hold her? You know not to drop her or nothing? All right. You hold her, and I'll get the pop cans. I'll be right back.

CARLOS: Coca-cola.

MONICA: Right on, loco-man.
(She hands off the baby and exits.)

CARLOS: Baby cry. Don't cry, baby. Carlos loves the baby.
(He shows the baby to LA LLORONA.)
Baby pees. Pee-pee.
(Eagerly, LA LLORONA reaches for the baby but MONICA re-enters with a sack of empty soda cans.)
Coca-cola

MONICA: You got it. You give me the baby, and I'll give you the bag. Not exactly what you call a fair trade, but fuck it, right?

CARLOS: Fuck it.

MONICA: Cool.
(They trade.)

CARLOS: Bye-bye, baby.

MONICA: Bye-bye you crazy whacko man.

(TITO enters)

TITO: Carlos, man, you guys having a party?

CARLOS: Pee on my hands?

TITO: Hey, that's all right, buddy, not today.

MONICA: He means the baby peed on his hands.
        (CARLOS nods.)

TITO: Cool. I'm really happy for you, man.
        (He claps CARLOS in the back and CARLOS exits, looking happily at his hands.)

MONICA: How come you ain't in school?

TITO: That baby might stop crying, you change her diaper or something.

MONICA: You got money to buy some?

TITO: You serious? What happened to David?

MONICA: You tell me. He's your brother.

        (TITO fumbles in his pocket and comes up with a roll of bills.)

TITO: How much they cost?

MONICA: Where'd you get that?

TITO: You want it or not?

MONICA: Tito, you ain't got no job.

TITO: You want it or not?

(MONICA takes the money.)

MONICA: I hope you ain't doing nothing stupid, Tito.

TITO: Nah, I'm just selling my chill pills.

MONICA: Your hyperactivity things?

TITO: It's like speed, only clean. They don't work that way for me. They slow me down. But I'm like backwards. But if you took them, you'd fly.

MONICA: No wonder you're flunking everything. You're all backwards and shit.

TITO: So? I'm making money. Vanessa gets diapers. I'm gonna get a car.

MONICA: What are you gonna do with a car?

TITO: Drive it, stupid. I don't know. Go on a date.

MONICA: You looking for a girlfriend, Tito? Who's gonna do you?
(ANDREA enters.)

TITO: Hey, Dre. Ain't you supposed to be in school?

ANDREA: Look who's talking.

TITO: Yeah, but you're a poetry genius and shit.

MONICA: And your dad's Rudolfo Cuesta and he eats girls who skip school for breakfast. Oh. Maybe you're meeting your man?

ANDREA: I haven't seen him.

TITO: Hey, did he do something to you, Dre? Are you all right and all?

ANDREA: (To MONICA.) Is Tia awake?

MONICA: Yeah, she ain't too doped out yet.

TITO: Why don't you hang with us, Dre?

ANDREA: I need to talk to Tia.

MONICA: (Calling after.) The Incredible Crying Baby and Ass Backwards Boy, Drea. Don't leave me all alone with this fun.

TITO: Some two-bit rodeo rider with a black truck and she's like a different person.

MONICA: Who you think she should be with, Tito? You?

> *(Lights fade on them and they exit as ANDREA approaches TIA.)*

ANDREA: Are you asleep?

TIA: Am I ever really awake?

ANDREA: Tia. I have been seeing a boy.

TIA: Un novio? What is his name?

ANDREA: Gilberto Irevedra. He came with the rodeo last month.

TIA: You are bringing him to meet the family soon, I hope?

ANDREA: Papa won't let me have a boyfriend.

TIA: There is wisdom in this. You are young, mi'ja.

ANDREA: How old were you the first time you were … with a man?

TIA: Diez. Quisas once.

42

ANDREA: Eleven?

TIA: I did not ask for it. I was late coming home from the fields and he took me behind the arbors. Since then, I can never eat grapes, even the smell is frightening. Bees buzzed and he sweated all over my dress. Afterwards I could not walk, my legs were all stretched out. I thought I had been very bad, when all the time it was this man, sí? But we blame ourselves first, always.

ANDREA: Did you bleed?

TIA: Yes. All women do, the first time. The men break something inside of you. But why these questions, hija? How far have things progressed with this novio of yours?

ANDREA: Tia, he wanted me to—

TIA: Oh, mi madre. Say no more.

ANDREA: But—

TIA: But nothing. Men are like monkeys, rubbing themselves up against trees, walls, any girls they can find. But you must not listen to him, Andrea. He will try everything he can think of, but you must resist.

ANDREA: But what if I love him? And he loves me?

TIA: A truly honorable man would not get you into trouble. You see this, do you not?

ANDREA: But it can't happen the first time.

TIA: Oh, but it can. First time, last time, anytime. Believe me. It is the easiest thing in the world to make a baby.

ANDREA: (Pause.) How do you know there is a baby inside you?

TIA: Estas embarazada? Are you with child?

ANDREA: I don't know. And since we … Tia, he has not called me since we …

TIA: Oh, carita.

ANDREA: What did I do wrong?

TIA: What is done is done, mi'ja. Wrong or right it is done.

ANDREA: He will come back.

TIA: Andrea.

ANDREA: He will come back and I will bring him here to meet you. My novio.

TIA: That would please me more than you could imagine. But you must tell your father if there is something--something wrong—

ANDREA: I can't! I can't, Tia—you know how he--

TIA: Then you come to me and we will tell him together. You come to me, Andrea. If there is something wrong.

ANDREA: Don't worry, Tia.

TIA: It can happen anytime, chica. It can happen anytime.
(Lights up on PAPA, making a speech to the Neighborhood Council. He wears his uniform. ANDREA crosses to sit next to him as he talks. Lights remain on TIA.)

PAPA: The last thing on our agenda this evening involves renovations to our neighborhood recreation center. The City Parks and Recreation Department tells me they cannot divert funds to renovate the building at this time. They would prefer to tear down the building instead. The City Council seems to believe that our children can be served just as well by the recreation center at Forest

44

Hills. When I asked the Council how our children were supposed to transport themselves to Forest Hills, they had no reply. When I explained that, for obvious reasons, our children were reluctant, even frightened to cross into another neighborhood to play, I received blank stares and shrugs. To them, one park is as good as another. So if we are to save our community center, we must take responsibility ourselves. I do not need to tell you how vitally important it is that our children have a safe, supervised, clean place to play, right here where we live. My daughter Andrea will pass out a petition for you to sign. It says, simply, that we would like our neighborhood recreation center to stay open at all costs. Also, I am asking for volunteers, to help raise funds, to go to meetings. I understand if we can form our own nonprofit company, we may take over the renovations of the building ourselves. If there is anyone who has time to help, it would mean so much to the children. Please. What can you do to save the children? Thank you for your time. Good night.

(ANDREA and PAPA exit. TIA, high on morphine, rocks in her chair. LA LLORONA hums nearby.)

TIA: It can happen anytime. Anytime. Anytime. Anytime.

(MONICA enters.)

MONICA: Who are you talking to?

TIA: I am talking to the Lady.

MONICA: You sure Loco Carlos ain't your long lost brother?

TIA: You have been out all night.

MONICA: So?

TIA: You're going to get into trouble again, you keep playing around like that.

MONICA: I'm already in trouble, eh? Where's Andrea?

(TIA shrugs, rocking. TITO enters, sleepy-eyed, the baby in one arm.)
Tia? Where are the children?

TIA: What children?

MONICA: Tia, your children. Where's my baby?

TITO: It's cool. I got them up. They went on the school bus.

MONICA: Why didn't you go?

TITO: You want me to leave Vanessa alone with the morphine queen?

MONICA: You respect your mama, pendejo.

TITO: I couldn't find no milk, so I like soaked Frankenberry in water and she liked it okay. Didn't you, carita?

MONICA: Dang Tito. You don't know nothing about babies.
(She snatches the baby away and begins fussing over her frantically.)
What happened to Drea?

TITO: She got sick and sick and sick. Throwing up all over the place. Like five times. I said, "Go home or we're gonna catch whatever you got and then the whole house'll be swimming in puke." And mama, she got no white blood cells right now—

MONICA: You put the children to bed?

TITO: You see anyone else here? Mama was asleep.

MONICA: You dosed her too much.

TITO: I didn't. I did like the nurses said. But Monica, everything hurts her, man. What do you want me to do? I didn't want to bother her and I took care of things. So you could have a good time.

46

MONICA: Shit. (Pause.) The baby, she looks okay. You did okay.

TITO: Is David coming home?

MONICA: He got a construction job on the rez. This was his last night in town.

TIA: You stay out all night, you're going to get pregnant.

MONICA: Tch. I already am pregnant.

TITO: What you want to have another baby for?

MONICA: Shut up, Tito. You may be the man in this house, but you're still just a boy, you don't talk to me like that.

TITO: I watch your kid so you can fuck David all night—

MONICA: (Smacks him.) Shut up, I said. (To TIA.) You're not saying anything.

TIA: What should I say? Will you quite school?

MONICA: I don't go anyway.

TIA: Who is the boy? David?

MONICA: It doesn't matter.

TIA: What do you mean? How can you get pregnant and not care about the boy who made you that way?

MONICA: I don't know. I don't know, okay? I just want to have another baby. I get pregnant, it doesn't matter how fat I am. I have a baby and people know some man loves me. Okay? All right?
     (She leaves the room.)

TIA: Go to school.

TITO: I don't want to go to school.

TIA: Get your books and go.
> *(Lights dim on TIA. We hear ANDREA crying. She sits in a heap on the floor outside DR PENNE's office. DR PENNE enters.)*

DR PENNE: Andrea? What are you doing in school so early?

ANDREA: I missed an appointment yesterday. I have been so busy …

> *(LA LLORONA sits at DR PENNE's desk.)*

DR PENNE: Are you all right?

ANDREA: I've been sick to my stomach.

DR PENNE: You look tired.

ANDREA: I'm … busy. What was the appointment about?

DR PENNE: The deadline for the National Scholastic Poetry Awards is coming up. Your English teacher passed some of your poems on to me. I think you should enter them, of course.

ANDREA: Oh.

DR PENNE: The prize is publication in a national journal. Can you see this in print? (Reads.)
You pluck them one after the other
Petals of the wild rose, la rosa del tierra
And como un niñita you sing as you pull

ANDREA: I don't—

DR PENNE: Él me desea, él no me desea—

ANDREA: Miss, I'm just not sure I should write anymore.

DR PENNE: I beg your pardon?

ANDREA: I am very worried.

DR PENNE: What is it?

ANDREA: I think … my cousin Monica … might be pregnant.

DR PENNE: Yes?

ANDREA: Is there … some kind of help for her … For her to …?

DR PENNE: We have a high school equivalency program for young mothers. She could call me and make an appointment. We do have a waiting list for the program. I'm trying to get a grant to expand, but—

ANDREA: So, if she got the equivalency—she could still go to college? Even with a baby?

DR PENNE: Well, I mean, yes, but it would be very difficult. Why are you worrying about this? Your cousin is not your responsibility.

ANDREA: Someone should help her.

DR PENNE: Well of course. But that's what her parents are for. That's what I'm for.

ANDREA: Her father is very strict.

DR PENNE: But that is her problem, right? Not yours?

ANDREA: Miss, it's just that—

>   (*LA LLORONA puts her hand on the phone. It rings. It continues ringing.*)

DR PENNE: I have to get that. I'm expecting an important call.

ANDREA: It's okay. I'll stop by later.

DR PENNE: Andrea. Don't worry about your cousin.

ANDREA: All right.

DR PENNE: Take the paperwork for the Scholastic Poetry Awards. Worry about that. All right?
> *(ANDREA takes the papers and moves away. DR PENNE answers the phone.)*

Michael. Michael. Hello? Hello? (Hangs up.) Well, shit.

> *(ANDREA crosses and kneels by a candle. She lights it and crosses herself and prays, as if in church. LA LLORONA follows her.)*

ANDREA:
Él me desea. Él no me desea.
For a little child, una niñita, a game
He loves me, he loves me not
Holy mother, make it a dream

> *(LA LLORONA takes the papers for the Scholastic Poetry Awards and destroys them, by ripping them up or burning them over the candle flame. Music.)*

TIA: There are so many songs and stories about these men. How they take you and then how they leave you alone each night, every night, seeking other women, other moons. It makes me tired to think of it.
> *(The MASKED MAN enters. He touches ANDREA's shoulder.)*

ANDREA: Holy father, help me to find him again. Make him love me. Please. Do you know what it is to love? I will give you whatever you ask, if he will only say he loves me.

(LA LLORONA laughs and takes the hand of the MASKED MAN and leads him away. ANDREA reaches, then gives up, and lies down, as if to sleep.)

TIA: It was as if she went to sleep. The days passed in meaningless succession. She was like one dead, waiting for his return. And she waited in vain.

(A burst of mariachi music. We are at the fiesta. LA LLORONA dances folklórico with the MASKED MAN, ESME dances with PAPA, MONICA with TITO. Only ANDREA hangs back. TIA puts on a pretty scarf and gets up from her chair to watch and clap. The dance ends just as DR PENNE enters.)

DR PENNE: Esmeralda!

ESME: Miss, you decided to come to our fiesta. I am so glad. Come, you can meet my tia.

DR PENNE: She's here? I thought she was very ill.

ESME: She would not miss this. It is her last one, and she wants to be with us. Did you have some food? We have everything. Do you wish to dance?

(She takes her hand leading her to TIA.)

DR PENNE: I don't know how. No one dances where I come from.

ESME: Do you like this dress? My mama made it. It is very traditional.

DR PENNE: It is lovely. All of this is lovely.

ESME: Tia, look, here is the Miss who got me into the science program. And she helped Andrea put her poem in the contest, too. She is bringing everything good to our school.

TIA: How do you do, Miss.

DR PENNE: How do you do. Esmeralda has told me so much about you.

ESME: I am going to go dancing, now!

> *(She runs to another part of the stage to talk to MONICA or TITO. The fiesta continues with music and maybe even some more dancing.)*

TIA: We are all so grateful for the help you have given our daughters.

DR PENNE: Well, I try. I guess I haven't been so successful with Tito.

TIA: Oh, Tito. He is too high-spirited to sit all day in a classroom. It is a hardship for all boys that age. What can anyone do?

DR PENNE: I've heard from the children that you are very ill.

TIA: It is bad and now it is better. But I am going to die.

DR PENNE: Oh, I'm … oh, I'm so sorry.

TIA: You break it down into minutes. This is a good minute. Is it not?

DR PENNE: It's … very nice, yes.

TIA: My whole family is here. Esmeralda said you would bring your husband and children to our fiesta.

DR PENNE: She must have been mistaken. I'm not married.

TIA: No? Never?

DR PENNE: Never.

TIA: No children?

DR PENNE: No. There are certainly a lot of children here, though.

TIA: Yes. You have family in town here?

DR PENNE: I don't. My family lives across the country.

TIA: But this must be very hard for you.

DR PENNE: I, uh. I never looked at it that way.

(PAPA, out of breath from dancing, enters.)

PAPA: I am getting too old for this nonsense.

TIA: Rudolfo, you are never too old.

PAPA: (To DR PENNE.) You are the counselor from the school.

DR PENNE: Ellen Penne.

PAPA: It is nice to see you here.

DR PENNE: Esmeralda invited me.

PAPA: Ah. Well. Have you had something to eat?

DR PENNE: I am fine, thank you. Tell me. Is Andrea feeling any better?

PAPA: Andrea. Better than what?

DR PENNE: Well, you know she's been missing so much school. I wondered if—

PAPA: Andrea has been missing school?

DR PENNE: Well, yes. I mean, she's missed some appointments with me and when I do see her she tells me she's not been feeling well and I ...

PAPA: I did not know this. Excuse me please, one moment.
(He approaches ESME.)
Esmeralda where is your cousin Andrea?

(ESME indicates she doesn't know. He talks to others and eventually exits. Meanwhile, DR PENNE stares after him at a loss.)

DR PENNE: Okay. Maybe you could show me where the food tables are.

(TIA leads her off. ANDREA enters. TITO catches sight of her and approaches.)

TITO: Ain't you dancing?

ANDREA: I don't feel like dancing.

TITO: You don't feel like doing nothing anymore, little Dre. C'mon. You like my shirt?

ANDREA: It's very bright.

TITO: You sick again? You want me to get you some soda? Drea?

(GILBERTO enters.)

ANDREA: Never mind.

TITO: Dre, listen—

(She ignores him, but TITO hangs back, watching.)

GILBERTO: Hey, little girl.

ANDREA: Where have you been? What happened to you?

GILBERTO: Nothing. I just got things to do, you know. Rodeo season starts up north in a few weeks. I had to set some things up. You look good.

ANDREA: You're going away again.

GILBERTO: Babe. My knee is almost better. Hey. Maybe we could be alone, eh? I got my trucked parked down the street.

ANDREA: What do you mean?

GILBERTO: Didn't you miss me?

ANDREA: Yes, I—

GILBERTO: (Closing in on her.) Because I missed being with you. I missed a lot of things.

ANDREA: You want to do it to me.

GILBERTO: Hey, I want to be close to you.

(He tries to lead her away but she pulls back.)

ANDREA: That's all you want to do.

(TITO is still hanging back but he calls.)

TITO: You okay, Dre?

GILBERTO: Leave us alone, why don't you. (To ANDREA.) Don't start that. Be sweet.

ANDREA: And then you will go away again and never—

GILBERTO: Hey. Hold on. I got my life, right? The world does not stop just because I make love to you.

ANDREA: Yes, it does.

GILBERTO: Tch. It's a big world, carita. You don't know nothing.

ANDREA: Teach me.

GILBERTO: You coming to my car, or what?

ANDREA: If I do, will you stay here with me? I give myself to you and in return—

GILBERTO: It doesn't work that way. I don't owe you something just because you let me—

ANDREA: Yes you do.

TITO: (Approaching.) You need help, Dre?

GILBERTO: (To ANDREA.) Why you got to be like this? You wanted it. Don't turn this around and make it like you didn't.

ANDREA: I gave myself to you, for you.

GILBERTO: And with a little more practice, you'll have it down.

> *(It takes a moment for this to sink in. Then she throws herself at him.)*

ANDREA: Hijo de puta!

> *(She continues yelling and punching.)*

TITO: What did he do?

ANDREA: I hate you! I hate you!

> *(She cries. TITO prevents GILBERTO from exiting.)*

TITO: What did you say to her?

GILBERTO: Nothing. She's loca.

TITO: What did you do to her?

GILBERTO: I didn't do nothing.

TITO: You did something to her.

GILBERTO: I'm outa here.

TITO: Not until you explain yourself.

ANDREA: Tito, get away from him; this is none of your business.

TITO: What did you do to her man?

> *(She tries to pull him away from GILBERTO. Bedlam, with TITO throwing punches, GILEBRTO defending himself and ANDREA in between them.)*

PAPA: (Off.) What is this?
> *(Entering, he makes quick work of breaking up the fray. He cuffs TITO and collars ANDREA. OTHERS enter to watch.)*
What is going on here?

GILBERTO: (Hands up.) Nothing you can't handle. (He exits.)

ANDREA: (Calling after.) Gilberto!

PAPA: Tito, what were you doing to your cousin?

TITO: I was trying to help her!

PAPA: Then why is she crying?

TITO: I don't know.
> *(PAPA grabs ANDREA, she struggles.)*

PAPA: What happened here, hija! Tell me.

DR PENNE: Mr. Cuesta, perhaps—

PAPA: What did you tell me? That she is missing school. And I do not know this. And then I find her—what—in some disturbance with Tito and…where has that man gone? Did he hurt you, mi'ja?

ANDREA: (Overlapping.) Tito, why you go crazy like that?

TITO: (Overlapping.) You're the crazy one. You were hitting him and shit--

ANDREA: (Overlapping.) I had to talk to him, and you—

PAPA: Stop this! Both of you!

ANDREA: I had to talk to him.

PAPA: Callate! I will not have you behaving this way.
      (Pointing to TITO.)
You I will deal with later.
      (TITO exits with an oath.)
What happened?

ANDREA: I was talking—I was talking to someone and Tito went crazy. Now may I be excused, please?

PAPA: No. What is this about school? Why are you missing school?

ANDREA: Papa, please.

PAPA: What lies have you been telling me?

ANDREA: Papa—

DR PENNE: Mr. Cuesta—

TIA: Rudolfo. Leave her to me. Callate. Estamos a la fiesta, con la familia. La hija esta muy jóven y muy delicada. Cálmate. Hay otras aqui, eh?

PAPA: Andrea, hija please. (To DR PENNE.) I am sorry. (To ANDREA.) Please tell me that you are not … that you-you cannot lie to me, hija—

TIA: Leave her to me, Rudolfo. Andrea, take me home. I am tired.

ANDREA: It is all right, Papa. I will take Tia home.

PAPA: Yes.
        (ANDREA exits with TIA He looks at DR PENNE.)
I am sorry for that scene.

DR PENNE: It's all right.

PAPA: You think I over reacted. Perhaps I did. (Beat.) Do you see what is around us? This fiesta, this music, this family. To me it is like something that rises up out of the earth and gives me strength. What we call fuerza. To have a stranger come in, who frightens my daughter, in the one place where she should be safe. Here. This was a good place when I was a boy. And now I am afraid for my daughter. I don't know what to do.

DR PENNE: I wish I had answers for you, Mr. Cuesta. But I am a stranger here, too.

PAPA: Yes. But you mean well.

        (Lights up on MONICA, ANDREA and ESME with TIA. TIA dozes, MONICA has a shampoo or lotion container that is a tube.)

MONICA: You mean you haven't read it in a book?

ESME: I don't read those kind of books.

59

MONICA: My cousin Nita showed me how when I was thirteen. So first, you should wear the kind of lipstick that don't come off, because he likes to look down and see your mouth like a puta's all red and wet.

ESME: He does?

MONICA: Men like to look at stuff. What do you think all the magazines are for, eh? Tch. Okay. This is really important. You have to stretch your lips over your teeth, so you don't accidentally nick it or nothing. That's the main thing. Bite it, and you're dead.
(She holds out the lotion bottle to ESME.)
You try it.

ESME: It's this big?

MONICA: If you're lucky. Go on. Try it.

ESME: No.

> *(ESME passes the bottle to ANDREA, who laughs in spite of herself and shakes her head.)*

MONICA: It's mostly like an up and down kind of thing with your head, right? Lips over your teeth and up and down and—

ESME: Gross!

MONICA: I know. I was like, "Dang, Nita. I'm not going to stick some guy's dick in my mouth" and she was like, "Well, you want to get pregnant or what then?"
(ANDREA stops laughing but the others do not notice.)
And I am like, "well I am not going to do that." Besides, around here it's like a badge of honor. It's a gift you give him, his child. But then I heard that stuff is good for your skin? Like, if you jack him off or give him a blow job you can rub it on your face and it will clear up your zits and stuff. If Nita'd told me that, I might done it sooner, right?

(ANDREA gets up and crosses to TIA.)
Did I offend you or something, Dre?

ANDREA: Why does she keep sleeping?

ESME: They upped the morphine.

MONICA: So what's the dirtiest thing you ever did with Gilberto? Truth.

ANDREA: I don't know.

MONICA: Come on! Spill. It's not like he's here getting his feelings hurt. Did you even touch it?

ESME: Monica, shut up! Can't you see she don't want to talk about it? (Pause.) Right, Dre? You were too good for him.

ANDREA: I got too much to do anyway.

MONICA: Yeah. She's got so much to do. She's got the Neighborhood Association Bake Sale and the Poetry For White People Society. Tch. You had a kid, you'd know what busy really is.

ESME: Monica! (To ANDREA.) I know you really loved him.

ANDREA: You don't know nothing, Esmeralda.

ESME: Okay. Maybe I don't. But I know if I read something, or do some homework, I feel better. Maybe if you wrote a poem—

MONICA: Yeah. Every time I feel bad I do a little Algebra.

ESME: I'm going to bust your face, Monica.

MONICA: Try it.

ANDREA: Tia, wake up.

ESME: Drea …

ANDREA: She's going to die and who am I going to talk to?

ESME: Why don't you talk to us?

ANDREA: What do you two have to tell me? How to read a book? How to suck cock?

    (She exits. ESME turns to MONICA.)

MONICA: What are you looking at?

ESME: I'm not looking at anything, Monica. I'm not looking at a stinking thing.

    (In another part of the stage TITO, who holds a comic book, talks to CARLOS, who sorts and crushes pop cans.)

TITO: No way, Carlos. His skeleton ain't made of aluminum. It's made of ademantium. And nothing can crush it. Those claws he got? They're stronger than diamonds.

CARLOS: Diamonds.

TITO: Wolverine is the shit, man. Look.

    (CARLOS looks at the comic book.)

CARLOS: Pretty lady.

TITO: That's Jean Gray. He's always had a crush on her, but she likes another guy. She's like got mind control and she's really smart and everything and he's this bad ass guy with claws and a really bad temper. And what's a girl like her gonna do with a guy like him, huh?

CARLOS: He could save her.

62

TITO: Right, crazy man.

CARLOS: I know you think I don't see. But Andrea. Tito. There is a ghost inside her eyes. And I have seen La Llorona, she has told me—

TITO: Let's take the cans to the center, okay Carlos—

CARLOS: Someone should save her.

TITO: I know. But I'm not Wolverine. I'm like you. I'm a mutant with no superpowers.

CARLOS: The lady cries.

TITO: You think I don't know that? Come on, Carlos.

(They exit. In another part of the stage DR PENNE is on the telephone.)

DR PENNE: What kids? I'm too busy on the phone trying to get my grants to actually help any kids. Let me tell you something Michael, bureaucracy was invented to keep us busy trying to help people, but never actually changing anything. I can't think. I can't feel.
        (Lights up on TIA.)

TIA: After a time, she ceased to feel. One day he came to her after being away for so long. And he said, "I do not want you. I have someone else. But I want the children. You give me our children for they are mine." But she turned her head away and would not look upon him.

DR PENNE: I wish you could have been there, Michael. And seen those kids. And the music and dancing and costumes.

TIA: He had made his wishes known at last. He was through with her. And soon she could hear only one note in her head, only one line of a song. One idea.

DR PENNE: That's a fabulous idea! The City Council just needs to see them, meet them. If they did, if they knew how extraordinary they are, they would open up their coffers. They don't need numbers. They need people. They need to see the kids.

TIA: What to do with the children. What to do with the children. She must not give him the children.

(ESME and MONICA enter screaming at one another as the lights fade on TIA and DR PENNE.)

MONICA: Bitch! You fucking bitch!

ESME: You got no right to call—

MONICA: Summer school? Are you shitting me?

ESME: You can't learn Calculus in one semester, okay? I got to study over—

MONICA: No! Goddammit. You think I don't know what you're up to? Go to school so you don't have to deal with the shit that's in my face twenty four fucking hours a day. A little extra special school for extra special Esmeralda. Fuck y—

ESME: I'm just going to school! Why are you yelling at me?

MONICA: My time's up. No more benefits. I got to get a job. But when am I going to work? I got to take care of Tia. I got to take care of the baby. I work the graveyard shift somewhere, maybe? And how am I going to get there? Walk? In the middle of the night?

ESME: What do I do about that?

MONICA: I don't know. You going to hide in the classroom until Tia dies?

ESME: Is she so much worse?

64

MONICA: Yes, she's worse. What you think, stupid?

ESME: Mama did not say she was worse.

MONICA: Of course not. You are going to college. You are la flora blanca, la chica perfecta—

ESME: Monica—

MONICA: A job! A job! Chinga! All the jobs I qualify for are jobs for assholes. Count this. Sweep that. Put this plastic part into that plastic part. They look at me in these interviews and all they see is some fat, lazy cholita cow, I can see it in their eyes.

ESME: You know Monica, you finish high school you wouldn't have this problem.

MONICA: Listen to the vendida. Listen to the white girl. What do you know, Esme?

ESME: I know better than to get pregnant by a man who cares nothing—

MONICA: Bullshit! You can't even get a man!

ESME: And you lie around watching television all day when you could—

MONICA: Lesbiana. Vendida. Puta blanca!

ESME: You are the whore.

MONICA: What do you know? Your mama loves you! She kisses you and hugs you! She tells you that you are smart and pretty! She works her fingers to the bone so that you can have it good. Vendida bitch. What do you know? They throw me out of the house and I have to live here. Do you think I wanted this?

ESME: Monica, I don't know what—

MONICA: I just want to feel safe.

ESME: Wake up why don't you? A woman alone with two babies is not safe. You going to just keep getting pregnant and crying about it forever?

MONICA: Not everyone can be perfect like you. Let me tell you something. A man making love to you is yours. In the world, he goes out, he's got a job, he's got friends, he's got a car. But if he's inside you, he ain't going nowhere as long as it lasts. That's what I want. That's what I want. I just want him to stay. Every time they do me, I think, maybe this time he'll stay.

ESME: I am not perfect, Monica.

MONICA: Yeah right.

ESME: I am angry all the time.

MONICA: What do you got to mad about?

ESME: I don't know. Nothing. Everything. The world. Look at me. I yell at you when I should be helping you. Monica, I am sorry.

MONICA: Tia is dying and I am all alone in this house, facing it every day. Help me, Esme. Can you help me?

ESME: Of course.

(They embrace. ESME strokes her hair.)

MONICA: I used to be really good in soccer. Beck in sixth grade, I was the fastest girl in the neighborhood. All the boys wanted me to play with them. Then one summer, I got boobs and a butt and I couldn't run as fast no more. It seemed like all the boys wanted to do was watch my titties bounce. They didn't ask me to play goalie, even. You think the answer to everything is school. One day you're going to wake up and see. Life happens somewhere else. Here. This is life. This is life, chica.

(Lights fade on them. Lights up on ANDREA.)

ANDREA: I am the resurrection and the life. Believe in me.

(LA LLORONA enters, still in her mask, and puts on a lab coat, becoming a nurse.)

LA LLORONA: Andrea Cuesta.

ANDREA: I am the life.

LA LLORONA: Would you come with me, please? How are you today?

ANDREA: I am afraid there is something wrong with me.

LA LLORONA: We'll ask you some questions and we will find out, okay? What was the first day of your last period?

ANDREA: I can't remember. A long time ago.

LA LLORONA: How many months?

(TITO enters from another part of the stage. He carries on a different conversation with ANDREA, unaware of the other one she is involved in.)

TITO: You're getting fat.

ANDREA: I think I might have cancer.

TITO: What happened to you? You win some poetry prize, you turn into a blimp?

LA LLORONA: I'm sure that's not the problem.

(LA LLORONA takes ANDREA's blood pressure. PAPA enters and starts a separate conversation with ANDREA, who now must divide her attention between three competing voices.)

TITO: What are you eating all the time for?

ANDREA: Go away. Go bother someone else.

PAPA: What are you wearing? You look like a gangster.

LA LLORONA: Blood pressure normal.

> *(She looks in ANDREA's ears, throat, takes pulse, etc., over the rest of the lines.)*

ANDREA: It's a style, Papa. Nothing to worry about. You worry too much.

TITO: Got no one else to bother, baby. Everyone else is at baseball practice.

ANDREA: Why don't you go?

PAPA: You have never concerned yourself with style before.

TITO: I got summer school. I flunked three classes.

LA LLORONA: Your age?

ANDREA: I just turned sixteen.

PAPA: As long as you are not getting into gangs, mi'ja—

ANDREA: Really. These are just comfortable clothes.

PAPA: Is anything wrong?

ANDREA: My tia has cancer.

LA LLORONA: What kind of cancer?

PAPA: I expect you to be at the neighborhood association meeting—

ANDREA: It started in her female parts. But it has spread to her liver and her blood. She won't go to the doctor anymore. She is at home; we are making her comfortable. She wants to die.

TITO: Why don't you get out? Do something? Stop eating?

ANDREA: Get out, Tito!

PAPA: Your final grades were lower than usual, hija. Don't start getting lazy.

ANDREA: I'm so tired all the time.

TITO: You okay?

LA LLORONA: So there is a history of cancer in your family?

ANDREA: I don't know.

LA LLORONA: Are you taking any medication?

PAPA: Have you been lying to me, hija?

TITO: You gonna have another Ho-Ho?

ANDREA: No.

PAPA: Hija. Answer me. You do not turn your nose up when I ask you a question.

TITO: What do you want his phone number for? He don't want you.

LA LLORONA: Have you had sex in the last twenty four hours?

ANDREA: No. Please…

PAPA: I work my ass off for you. And you sulk at me and give me attitude—

ANDREA: Papa, I don't know what else to do—

PAPA: God help you if you turn out to be another teenage drop out, Andrea. I will not allow it.

ANDREA: I love you so much. Do you love me? Do you?

PAPA: I will not allow it. (Exits.)

LA LLORONA: I am going to leave you alone and I would like you to take off all your clothes, including your underpants and bra. Then put this cloth on you to cover yourself. The doctor will be right with you. (Exits.)

ANDREA: Help me.
        (Looks helplessly at the cloth and lets it drop.))
Let us say I dreamed it all. Let us say it is a dream.

        (Lights change. They are in TIA's house. TIA dozes.)

TITO: I don't even know why I try to talk to you.

ANDREA: Who is asking you to, Tito?

TITO: You used to be cool, Dre. Now you're like some—

ANDREA: Don't talk to me about what I am like.

        (She crosses to TIA.)

ANDREA: When is the last time she had a bath?

TITO: I don't know.

TIA: Is it time for more medicine?

TITO: That's all she cares about.

ANDREA: That's because she's in pain.

TITO: She's a ghost, just like you.

ANDREA: You don't know anything, Tito.

TITO: Maybe I do. Maybe I don't. Maybe I know where Gilberto is.

ANDREA: What?

TITO: Maybe I know someone who saw him at the Prescott rodeo.

ANDREA: What do I care?

TIA: Is it time for my medicine?

ANDREA: Not yet, Tia. How about I clean you and make you more comfortable?

TITO: Drea, he was never no good. Don't you know that? He just left you.

ANDREA: Go away, Tito.

TITO: Open your eyes.

ANDREA: Get out of here, so I can clean her.
        (TITO exits.)
Tia, there is something wrong.

TIA: Mi'ja. Why are your eyes filled with tears?

ANDREA: I'm frightened. Tia, I am going to have a baby and I don't know what to do.

TIA: How can you have a baby? You are just a little girl.

ANDREA: I have to go away. Before Papa finds out.

TIA: Where will you go?

ANDREA: Anywhere. Anywhere. Is there family in Mexico--

TIA: Oh, hija. It is so much more difficult there. Better to have your children here as I did.

ANDREA: I'm worried it is close to my time.

TIA: It must be time for my medicine.

ANDREA:You remember when I was sick to my stomach all the time?

TIA: It was so for me. Sicking everything up.

ANDREA: I went to the doctor, but I was so afraid, I ran away.

TIA: I too went to the doctor, and they tried to cut it out, but it was too far gone.

ANDREA: I don't want this to be happening.

TIA: They give me drugs for the pain. Give me my medicine. It's time.

ANDREA: I need you to help me, Tia.

TIA: Light a candle and pray. Let the candle burn and when it goes out, your prayer will be answered.

ANDREA: I have tried and tried to pray.

TIA: You must get more medicine. Or leave me alone.

ANDREA: Tia. It is Andrea. Don't drift away like this, please.

(In another part of the stage, DR PENNE speaks with ESME.)

DR PENNE: Esmeralda. Did we have an appointment today?

TIA: It must be time.

ESME: Hello, Miss. No, Miss.

TIA: Time for my medicine.

(Lights dim on TIA and ANDREA.)

DR PENNE: Is something wrong?

ESME: I … I think I must quit this program, Dr. Penne.

DR PENNE: No. You can't.

ESME: I—

DR PENNE: Esme. That would be a waste of your talents and potential—

ESME: Maybe right now that is not so important.

DR PENNE: What could be more important than your future?

ESME: The present. My family.

DR PENNE: Esmeralda, that's a nice sentiment—

ESME: It is not sentiment. It is not something in a greeting card, Miss. This is my heart. If I stay in this program, I am sitting in a room improving my mind while my aunt lies at home on her deathbed. I can take these courses next year, can I not, when things at home are more stable--

DR PENNE: There might not be an AP program next year, Esmeralda. The government is cutting education funding again, and this program will be the first to go, especially if you people keep dropping out.

ESME: What people? What do you mean?

DR PENNE: Look. The community here needs your example. I need your example, Esmeralda. I want … I want to take you to a city council meeting, as a school representative. I know if they meet you, they'll renew the funding, but if you drop out—

ESME: Is that what I am to you? Your token Mexican American Girl Genius?

DR PENNE: No. Of course not. But you are—Esme, am I supposed to just stand by while a brilliant young girl gives up her dream—

ESME: Yes, a dream. But only a dream. But my tia is real life. She is the rock of my neighborhood and when she is gone … a part of me will be gone as well. A part of all of us. I need to be home right now, for as long as it takes.
(She starts to exit the office.)

DR PENNE: Just a moment, Esmeralda, please—
(Her telephone rings. She is torn between the telephone and ESME. She answers the phone.)
Michael? Is that you?

(Lights out on DR PENNE as ESME bumps into TITO outside the office.)

TITO: Hey, alien breath.

ESME: Leave me alone.

74

TITO: Wait. Esme. Look. I don't want to say nothing, but I got to. Something is wrong with Andrea. She ain't acting right.

ESME: So talk to her about it.

TITO: I can't talk to her. My brain's backwards. I know. It's like a big fucking joke. But she's got this look in her eyes like she's already walking in a graveyard. The house is so whack man. And she's the Ghost of the Barrio and her dad is the Incredible Hulk and they're in a comic book, okay? And I am reading it but I can't talk to her. Because she thinks it's my fault that Gilberto went away.

ESME: Is it your fault?

TITO: He was a pendejo fuckhead, all right? He's gone because he just wanted her...I ain't gonna talk about that. I want you to do something.

ESME: Tito, you don't even make sense—

TITO: Esme. She don't even write poetry no more.

> *(In another part of the stage ANDREA talks on the phone. Lights up on GILBERTO, also on the phone. LA LLORONA is with GILBERTO.)*

GILBERTO: How the hell did you find me?

ESME: Why do I got to solve the problems of the world?

ANDREA: I just needed to talk to you.

TITO: Because no one else will.

GILBERTO: Okay.

ESME: I am sixteen years old.

ANDREA: Gilberto.

75

ESME: I can't fix anything.

GILBERTO: You talking to me, or what?

TITO: I hate you!

ESME: Jump off a bridge, Tito.

> *(She exits. Lights dim on TITO.)*

GILBERTO: Andrea?

ANDREA: I started getting sick and stuff

GILBERTO: Why are you telling me this?

ANDREA: Because I'm going to have a baby.

GILBERTO: No way. (Pause.) What do you want me to do?

ANDREA: I need your help.

GILBERTO: You want money?

ANDREA: I want to see you.

> *(LA LLORONA tugs at GILBERTO, kissing him and teasing him while he talks.)*

GILBERTO: I can't get away right now.

ANDREA: Then let me come live with you.

GILBERTO: I got nowhere for you to stay. I'm sleeping … on a couch.

ANDREA: I'm scared. I don't know what to do.

GILBERTO: You better not be thinking of getting rid of it.

ANDREA: How can I? I'm too far along.

GILBERTO: When is this baby due?

ANDREA: Did you already forget when we were together?

(LA LLORONA becomes more insistently distracting.)

GILBERTO: No. I just got a lot on my mind.

ANDREA: If my father finds out he'll kill me.

GILBERTO: Tell me what I can do for you, Dre.

ANDREA: I just … don't you want to talk to me?

GILBERT: I'm busy. Look, I'll send you some money, when I can. You take care of the baby, okay?

ANDREA: Please—

GILBERTO: I gotta go. This ain't my phone we're tying up.

ANDREA: Please.

GILBERTO: I gotta go. I really will send you money.

(He hangs up the phone, sweeping LA LLORONA into his arms.)

ANDREA: Let us say I dreamed it all.

(In another part of the stage, DR PENNE talks to TITO.)

TITO: I guess I really blew it, Miss.

DR PENNE: Tito, what were you thinking, walking on top of the perimeter fence?

TITO: Never mind.

DR PENNE: You could have been killed.

TITO: I know.

DR PENNE: Do you have no concept of consequences?
        (Silence)
Dr. Nuñez refuses to allow you back into summer school, Tito. I'm afraid you'll have to take all your classes over again in the fall.

TITO: Whatever.

DR PENNE: I assume your mother is still too sick to come and in and talk about this. (Silence.) I realize this is a hard time for you. I understand you are acting out. But also, Tito, I don't think this latest adjustment in your medication is working.

TITO: I got to tell you, Miss. I ain't been taking my medication.

DR PENNE: Without it, you cannot control your behavior.

TITO: I think it's whack, Miss. Take this pill. Take this program. It don't take care of the problem, okay?

DR PENNE: I see.

TITO: What do you do it for? What do you get out of this?

DR PENNE: I like helping young people.

TITO: Then how come you got her picture in the paper and then now you let her sit like some junkie on the couch, huh?

DR PENNE: Tito, are you talking about your mother—

TITO: And I want to hit something; I want to climb something; because—

DR PENNE: Calm down—

TITO: You don't see anything; nobody sees us!

DR PENNE: Tito, if you don't calm yourself I am going to have to ask you to leave. Sit. Down. I have had enough today. I realize you are upset about your mother—

TITO: I can deal with it! (He runs off.)

DR PENNE: (Following.) Tito! Tito, damn it!

> *(Lights up on ANDREA. She is trying to hurt herself, throwing herself on the floor, on the furniture, on set pieces.)*

TIA: I tell you the story. I tell it to you, but do you listen. The children. The children. That is all La Llorona wants. Even now she is howling outside your window, she is crying in the streets with sounds of gunshots and breaking glass all around her. She is there by your side, screaming for the souls of our children. And we hear her, oh I know we do. But we call ourselves innocent and unable. We stumble on the path and we do not look where we are going. And that is when she snatches the child—the child you have born, the child that is you, the child that is dying.

> *(LA LLORONA commands the stage as TIA hobbles off. Lights come up on DR PENNE, knocking on the door of TIA's house.)*

DR PENNE: Hello? Hello?

> *(ANDREA stops trying to hurt herself, because she is already hurting. She answers the door, trying to hide her pain.)*

ANDREA: Hello, Miss. I am surprised to see you here.

DR PENNE: Andrea. I … I didn't expect to see you either. I'm here about Tito. He became very upset in my office today and I thought … well, I should talk to your mother. May I speak with her?

ANDREA: She might not understand you, Miss.

DR PENNE: I can manage in Spanish.

ANDREA: She is not expected to last the week. It is close to the end.

DR PENNE: I see. (Pause.) Are you all right, Andrea?

ANDREA: I have … some cramps today. It hurts. It only just now got very bad.

DR PENNE: Are you alone here?

ANDREA: My cousin Monica will be here soon. And Esme. And mi papa. I am just … right now I am alone, but it is only now.

DR PENNE: You look very pale. Is there someone I can call?

ANDREA: My father has to give a presentation at the community center, but then he will come get me.
>   *(A contraction hits her. She breathes and tries to talk
>   through the pain.)*
I am sorry Miss. I am sorry that I…never sent my poems… to the contest…you wanted me to. Are you mad at me?

DR PENNE: Andrea. I … no.

ANDREA: Esme thought you were angry.

DR PENNE: No. I should … your father is at the community center, you said? I'm getting him—

ANDREA: No. Don't. Please. I am all right. Really.

DR PENNE: There must be something I can do for you. Is there anything? Anything at all?

> *(Pause. ANDREA starts to speak, but LA LLORONA puts a hand over her mouth, preventing her from saying a word.)*

DR PENNE : I don't think … You are not all right. I am going to get your father.
> *(DR PENNE exits.)*

ANDREA: No! Miss! Please!
> *(She staggers away and crouches alone, in deep labor.)*

Please don't get my father. I have to hide. And I can't scream. Gilberto. One. Two. Three. Let is say I dreamed it all. I can't feel my legs. My legs don't work at all. Don't scream. Mother of God. Madre de Dios. Maria, Maria, it hurts. It hurts. It hurts. I will hide. I will hide. And it will be a dream. Gilberto! Tia! It hurts. It hurts. Don't cry. Don't cry. It hurts. Make it a dream. Make it a dream. I. I. I am. I am, I am dreaming. Please. Please.

> *(Blackout. Lights up on an empty stage, morning. CARLOS enters, carrying something in his arms. ESME enters in another part of the stage.)*

CARLOS: Sleep. Sleep?

ESME: Carlos, have you been out all night again?

CARLOS: I look for Coca cola cans.

ESME: Oh, Carlos. I know.

CARLOS: Something is wrong.

ESME: You forgot to go to bed. Come on. I'll take you to your trailer.

CARLOS: I found her, Esmeralda.

ESME: What do you have?

CARLOS: And I was happy. But she is blue.

ESME: Okay.

CARLOS: And very cold. She will not get warm. Is she sleeping?
(He hands her the bundle and ESME drops it immediately.)
No. No. You must not drop her.
(He picks up the bundle.)

ESME: Carlos, put it down.

CARLOS: Is she sleeping? She does not cry.

ESME: Where did you find it?

CARLOS: In the trash cans.

ESME: Stay right here. Do not move. Even if you get tired, don't move. You … you keep her warm… while I find someone to help. Oh, God. Oh help! Help! Help me!

(She runs from the stage. CARLOS cradles the baby.)

CARLOS: Baby? Baby? Wake up baby.

(ANDREA sits with her hair in her face. MONICA kneels next to her.)

MONICA: La Llorona killed her children. That was her revenge. She took her children to the river and she held their faces underneath the water until their hearts stopped. And then she went crazy. She lived alone and she died alone and alone she went to the gates of heaven. And there God himself said to her … "Where are your children? How do you come here without your children? You must go back to the world and you must find them. Only then can you have rest."

(As guitar chords strum, LA LLORONA takes the baby from CARLOS's arms. MONICA sits in TIA's chair with her own baby. ESME enters and kneels by ANDREA.)

ESME: Drea? Drea?

CARLOS: Baby? Poor baby. (He exits.)

ESME: Drea, you have to start talking. Please. Tia is dead. I don't want to lose you, too. You cannot stay lost like this, in a dream. Drea. Did you kill her? They say that she was old enough to breathe on her own. Please. She was so small. I don't think you could have killed her. Oh, Drea, why didn't you tell us?

(TITO enters.)

TITO: Dang. I thought I fucked up.
    (ESME moves towards him.)
Feel like I'm in a silent movie. Like I'm walking on the moon. Ever since the funerals, I'm thinking how I got to start ninth grade again. So today, I took a pill.

ESME: It's getting dark, Tito. We better get home.

TITO: Or La Llorona find us?

ESME: Maybe.

(They do not move. Somewhere on stage LA LLORONA dances with her baby, she dances and dances.)

MONICA: I sometimes think if I could just buy a good car, you know? I could get out of here. But the really good cars only got room for two people and I like got more than that I want to take along. There ain't no Maserati with a kid seat. And no room in the back for toys. It's just you, cruising with the radio on. It's like, you gotta be cool, you gotta be alone. But I got too much stuff. And so I'm waiting on the porch watching all the cars go boy. And none of them are his.

TITO: You still going to be a doctor, Esme, and cure little kids and stuff?

ESME: It's a big job. And I'm just a nothing.

MONICA: (To her baby.) Go to sleep, little one.

TITO: I'm gonna be an astronaut. Right here. Right here by the river with the stars coming out.

MONICA: I will stay here with you, only you.

ESME: I just want to stay here awhile. Will you stay with me?

TITO: Esmeralda, man. I ain't going nowhere.

ESME: I know. I know.

> *(Lights dim slowly, the last thing we see is LA LLORONA with her baby.)*

AUTHOR'S NOTE

"La Llorona and Other Tales of the American Southwest" was first commissioned by Meg Nolan, Artistic Director of a.k.a. theatre in Tucson, AZ, in 1994.

It was subsequently developed at the National Playwrights Conference at the Eugene O'Neill Theatre Center in Waterford, CT, under the artistic direction of Lloyd Richards, with director Amy Saltz and dramaturg Israel Hicks, in 1997.

It received further development under the direction of Toni Press and with the help of Damesrocket Theatre in Tucson, AZ, in 1998.

I am deeply indebted to the above artists and institutions for their inspiration and guidance.

Heartfelt thanks is given, as well, to the many actors and technicians who helped bring "La Llorona" to life on the stage.
Thanks to them, the script received Honorable Mention in the Richard Hugo House Playwriting Awards in Seattle, WA, in 1999, and a Best Stage Play Award from the Moondance Film Festival in Boulder, CO, in 2003. A monologue from this script was published in Audition Arsenal, Volume 2, published by Smith and Kraus, in 2005.

Thanks also to the good folks at selfpubbookcovers.com, Rob and Shoshanna, and to artist yvonrz, who did such a great job with this book design.

And as always, thanks to my husband Keith, who is patient and supportive and unfailingly kind about all my endeavors.

www.ingramcontent.com/pod-product-compliance
Lightning Source LLC
Chambersburg PA
CBHW062115040426

42337CB00042B/2496